Selections from Harry Potter AND THE GOBLET OF FIRE ™

Music by Patrick Doyle

Except for
HEDWIG'S THEME by John Williams
MAGIC WORKS by Jarvis Cocker

CONTENTS

THE QUIDDITCH WORLD CUP
(The Irish)

Music by Patrick Doyle
Arranged by Dan Coates

HOGWARTS' MARCH

Music by Patrick Doyle
Arranged by Dan Coates

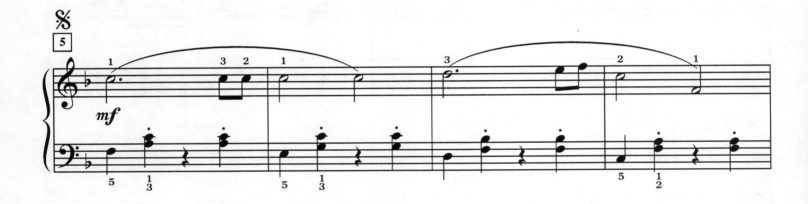

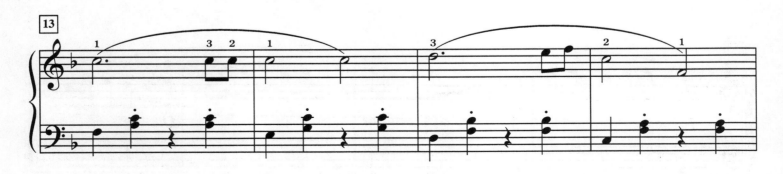

Fine

HOGWARTS' HYMN

Music by Patrick Doyle
Arranged by Dan Coates

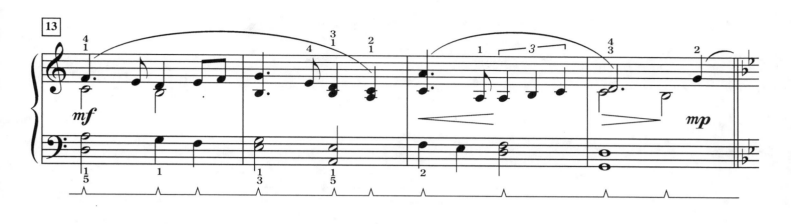

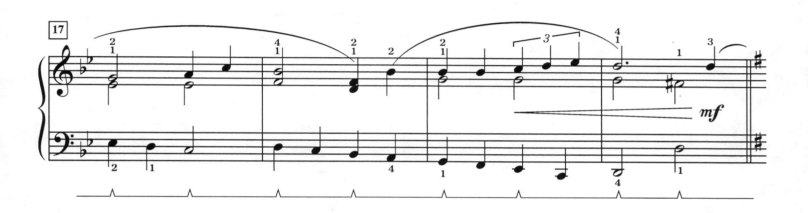

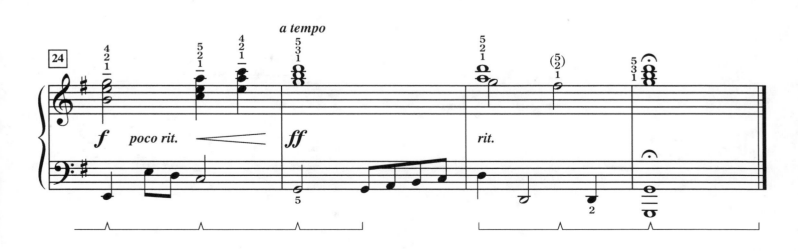

HARRY IN WINTER

Music by Patrick Doyle
Arranged by Dan Coates

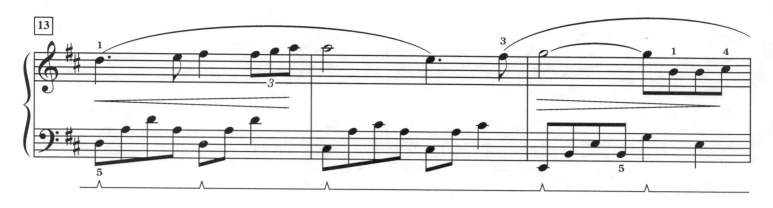

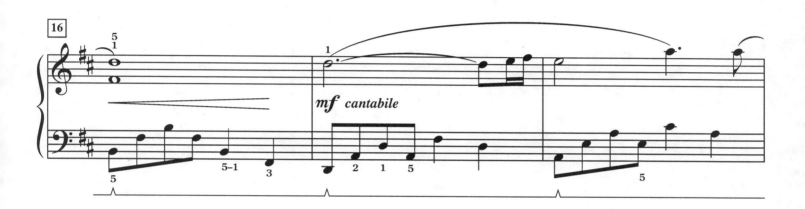

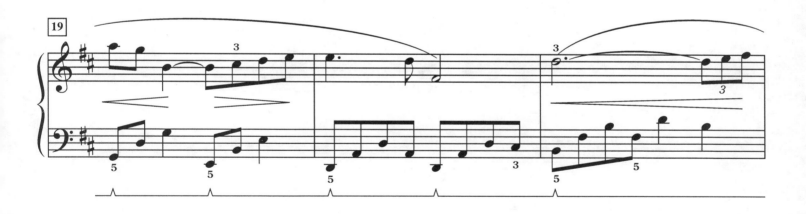

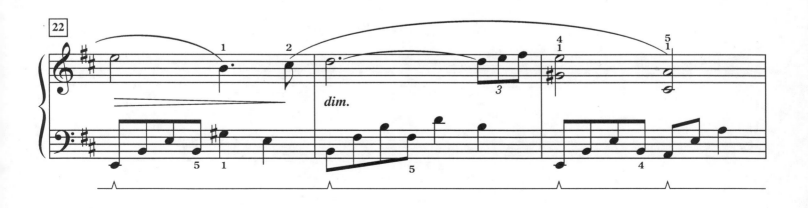

D.C. al Coda

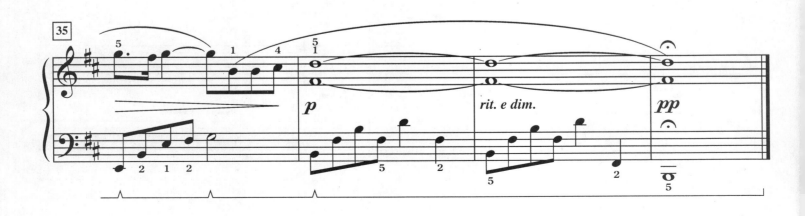

NEVILLE'S WALTZ

Music by Patrick Doyle
Arranged by Dan Coates

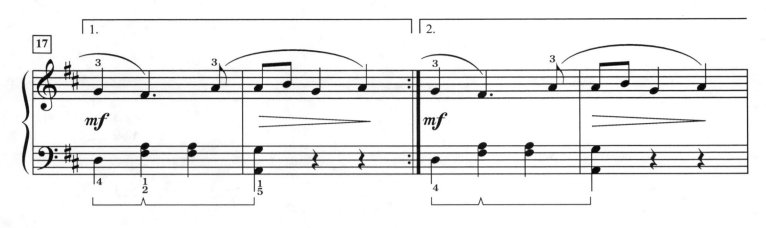

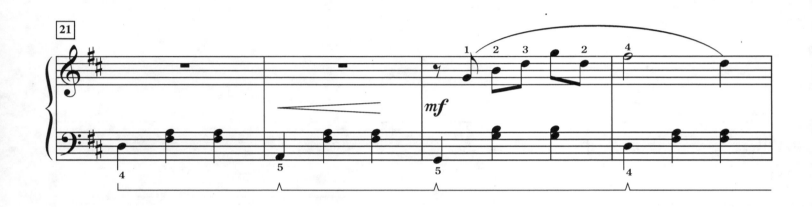

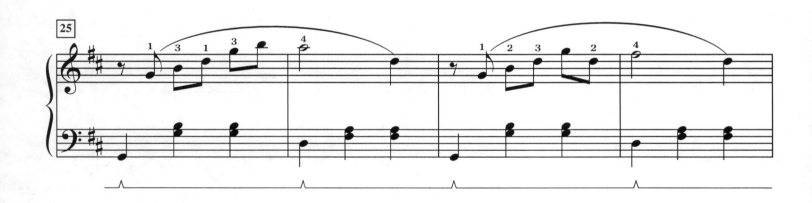

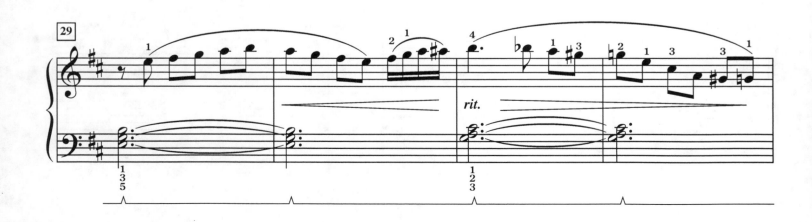

FOXTROT FLEUR

Music by Patrick Doyle
Arranged by Dan Coates

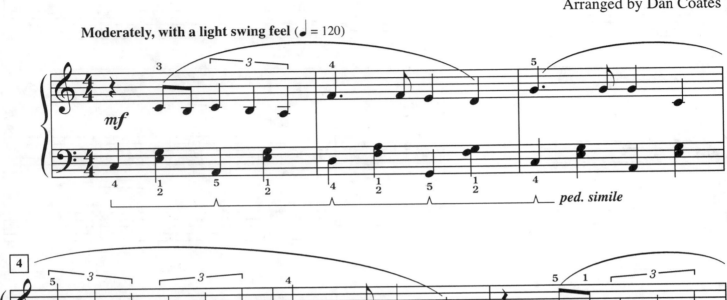

HEDWIG'S THEME

Music by **JOHN WILLIAMS**
Arranged by Dan Coates

MAGIC WORKS

By Jarvis Cocker
Arranged by Dan Coates

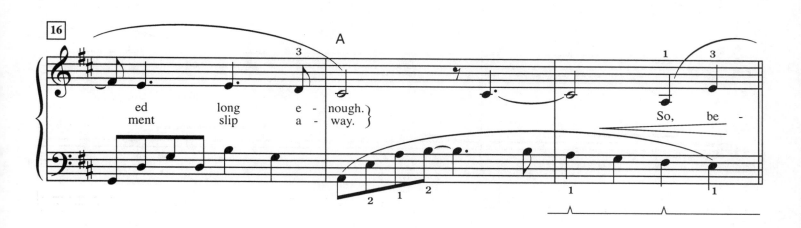

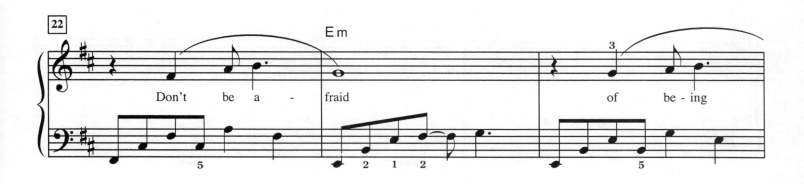

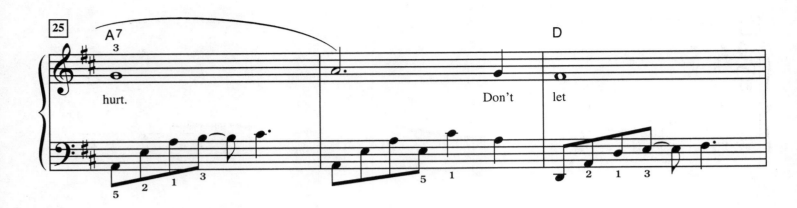

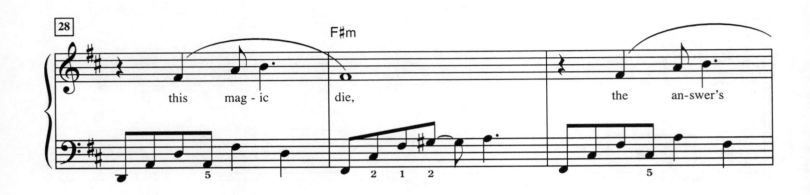

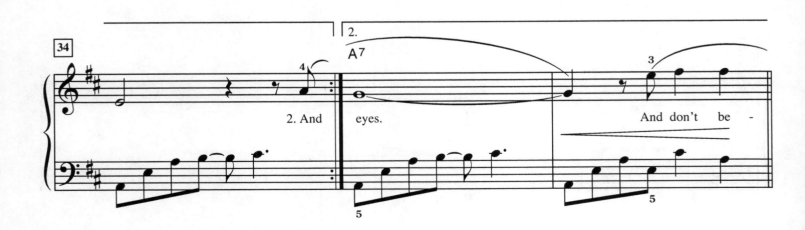

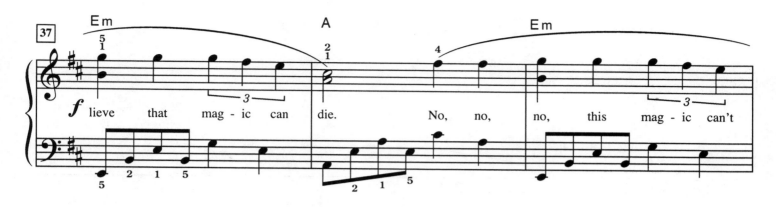

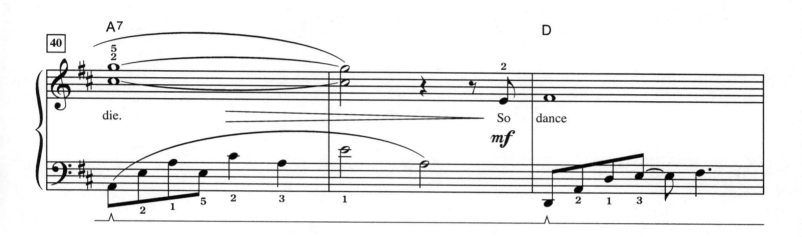

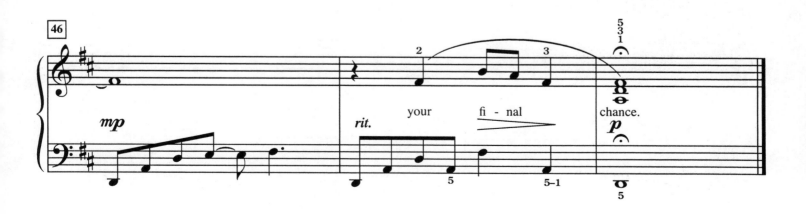

POTTER WALTZ

Music by Patrick Doyle
Arranged by Dan Coates

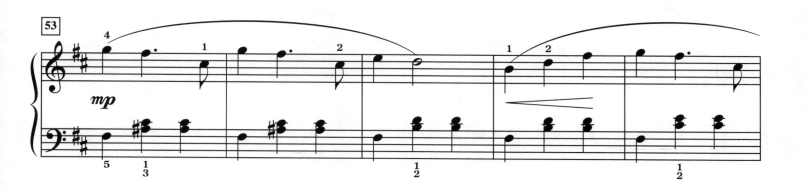

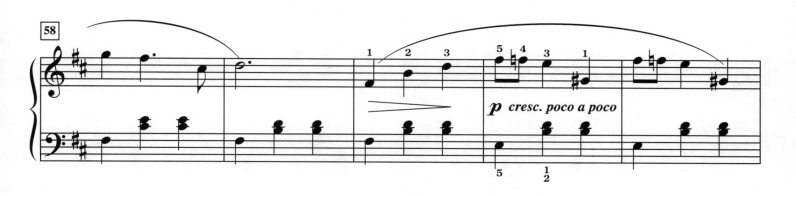

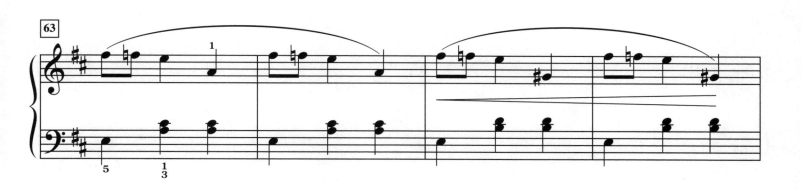

D.S. al Coda

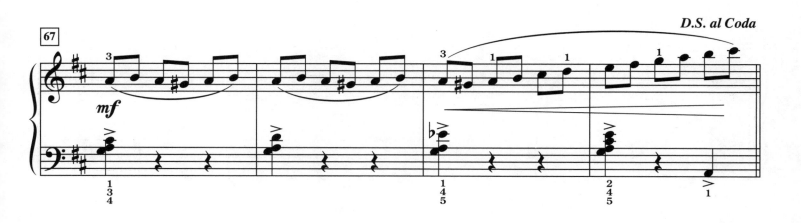

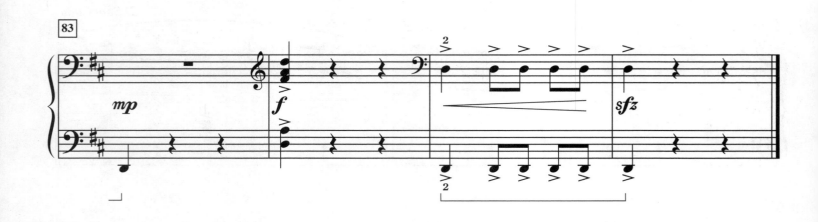